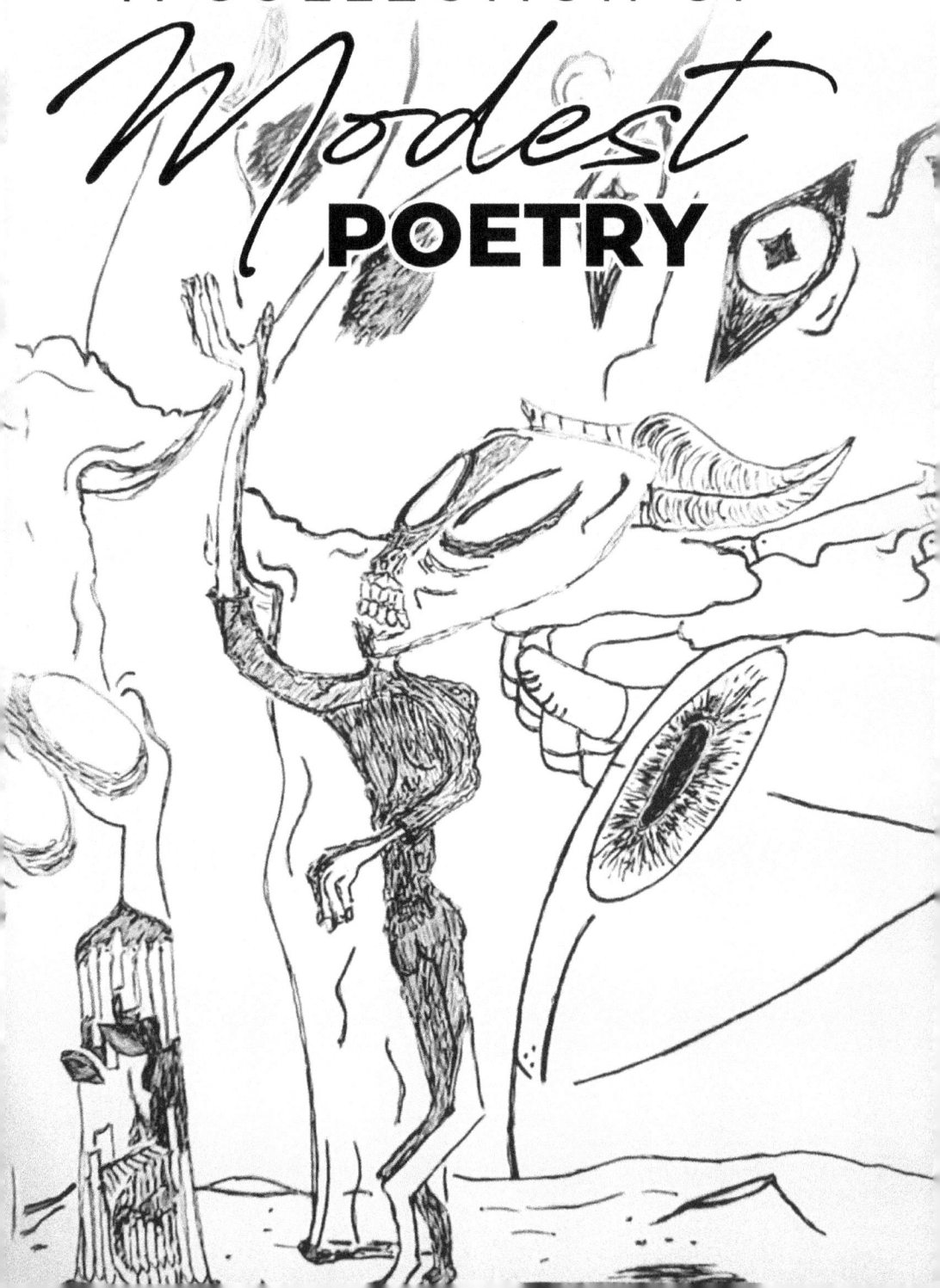

A COLLECTION OF

Modest

POETRY

A Collection of Modest Poetry

Copyright © 2024 by Noah Johnson.

MILTON & HUGO L.L.C.
4407 Park Ave., Suite 5
Union City, NJ 07087, USA

Website: *www. miltonandhugo.com*
Hotline: *1- 888-778-0033*
Email: *info@miltonandhugo.com*

Ordering Information:
Quantity sales. Special discounts are available on quantity purchases by corporations, associations, and others. For details, contact the publisher at the address above.

Library of Congress Control Number: 2024918074
ISBN-13:   979-8-89285-235-7   [Paperback Edition]
                  979-8-89285-236-4   [Hardback Edition]
                  979-8-89285-234-0   [Digital Edition]

Rev. date: 07/30/2024

Wonder along and think of simpler times, when Love was vast, and Divine with or without God.

Abstract

Imagine. Now Don't. Wonder along a wandering path that wonders itself into boredom. Imagination is key to understanding a lot of what makes something tick. Dreams carry us onto clouds, soft grass tends us to slumber, and mischievous beings dance into the foreground, all the while a red ball focuses into view as the sun purloins the horizon from our eyes, and we barely have the capabilities to ask why we are not blinking and not closing our burning eyes.

There is experience to be had in this life, gandered by the gleaners of what will last, blasts from the past carry us only so far until the moon itself must set and the sun to steal our play time away. So what are dreams, and what is nature? What are the ways that ebb and flow? What does it mean to take pride in being human? I thank the creator that I was born able to weep for the moth, I thank the universe for bearing its own weight down on me, for how else would I know I exist if not through the trepid rapids of glee and melancholy? God and Saints above the pain we feel is crucial to our extrapolations into why we know we exist, just as much as the joy we entangle ourselves in. What is this but an outcry at the joys of a life tranced with woe and drowned with joy and the gratitude someone so small couldn't possibly carry any further than the small of their back; where all tensions are held and stressors collapse.

Of My Own Nature

In the beginning there was silence.
The events that befell thereafter were chaos.
An immense transmogrification took place.
The Allusion of Chaos and the Dream of Life.
Everything in reality has its point of creation,
And this one here is mine.
Where once silently floating
Caressed by Vacuum.
Barren rock no more will I lay.
I take after too much our Ancestor Atoms.
Rending this horrid silence embracing the bold,
In creating something stupendous
To enrich the lives young and old.

Everyone has a beginning
And this one is mine.
You may not get it,
You may not now,
Yet soon you shall see it,
Soon you'll prowl
On knowledge as gifts to hook
You into seeing how one creates:
Worlds, Systems, Galaxies, Nebulae and Smiles,
Operates internally undrenched in their bowls.
A silenced voice echoing against choice is much
Like the comet or asteroid that came hurling down
That gave father earth a suspended feminine frown.

Both which grew stronger each man made year,
Though they were silenced and victim of sneer
They pressed on seeking peace
Till one day exhausted bound they plopped down withered and done.
Fed up with the bullshit of nearly everyone.
They began to write not for fun,

Such things are only imagined as a commodity only for ones.
No their ink stains in red,
An endless supply that comes straight from their head.
Their veins like railways,
For Chiron's shipping the dead.
Fast ahead are silhouetted shadows,
In silence they held rigid in stell,
Our cells fast at work.
Where once these gentle beings lived in Rye
Soon the conductor will run dry, so they
Pump and pump and pump s'more
Till all their words have dripped out
Making it more.

A beginning
A middle
An end.

And this one is mine.

Ode to Sleep Incarnate

Caress me, dear sweet dream bringer.
Hold me, softest hands that would e'er slink o'er the body—
My Body. Sometimes I deny you improperly through days on end.
Endless is my reckless and rambunctious behavior.
My dearly beloved I tried to close my eyes, and find most nights fulfilled
through that of your absence. I stand alone
droopy-eyed
arms outstretched.
Empty.
Fill this space, a hole in my heart for which your soul could cradle.
Let us find prosperity in blissful, delighted slumber.
Yet my human hands are weak, the desire that yearns with the heated
passions like that of the fires in tartarus; are too imprisoned as the Titans
within walls made of its own flesh.
The frivolities of my realities have consumed me to be
Heinous.
Deprived.
Monster of immoral proportions.
Yet weakened flesh continues to desire, be imprisoned, and conspire.
At your side will I at once soon reside, and when once my eyes begin to
close—
A meadow of wheat flourished before us, the horizon glimmering peace
in a destitute mind.

O' My Betrothed

I am.
I stand before you a sodden wretch
covered in mud, no longer fearful of the unknown.
Hiding those bits of mine given unto me at birth.
Today is asked of you as the sun rises.
I ask of you, Oh Wondrous Being of Creation that hath gleaned me from
my darkest pit.
I have hid away, forgotten to be nothing more than that of soil's shadow.
You have shown me mercy from the glistening light of agony.
You've breathed life into me once more and I cannot let this bestowal, this
gift go wasted.
I shall serve you, I shall follow you My Liege, My Lord, My Pharaoh, My
Shadow.
My Reason. I owe unto you My Deepest and most Vulnerable Form.
Upon your name I will even take. I will undo myself for you. Unravel my
flesh,
Peeling myself away like the skin of an apple, I whittle my being down to
its utmost weakest---
A beating heart, and two testicles.

Rebellium Sonnet

Upon a lonely soap box did they stand.
Limp and maimed one hobbles, stifles aloud,
"To Reap What Mother Earth Hath Gave Us!
Hide'n away is this Heap from the Crowd!"
The bodies convulse, no words, Silence fell.
The Proclamation of Freedom tranquillized.
Tho A Fire did ember from this husk's soul—
That made the living no more domicile.
We were drenched in Hope and in Blood.
For a Future we once had bequeathed—
Is Lost, Our sodden visage, Ghosts in Mud.
Dreams became inevitable Hiraeth.
If it's the limbs you want, you can have them.
I will find my peace in Rebellium.

Oh to Be a Bird

If I were to be a bird,
I'd want to float away,
Down on some river boat.
Un-Fluttering would I
Why fly when I can Ride
And steal myself for the 'venture?
With my swallow tunes I would provoke,
Young and Old folk to dance, and sing.
My hallow bones wouldn't need to move a wink.
And like the sirens of yore,
Before they'd even realize,
The horror in their eyes
I'd whisk my wings away,
as They'd sink to the bottom
in their shame.

Hope's Chastity

Oh to hope as one who is in a state of which one needs to hope,
I cannot hope to hope,
The expectancy of which belief is to ratify
—or rather–
gratify
but I will not adhear,
To the sodden visages which cry hail Mary,
hail Satan alike from their undignified prostration—
Neither exist in the capacity to listen.

An epiphany holds true to the skulls of classical notions

–hopelessness–

That perhaps to the notion of unhope,
the act of hoping not, for someone with saviorism.
Rather to break the shell,
slather the yolk
unto the dirty,
mud-dried,
Sun-baked stone–

a golden orbed expression of the unhope,
much like the dead it emulates a peace offering
yet to thy own countenance would claim,
Thusly,
Moreso—
not. Without an ignorant, pragmatic solution.

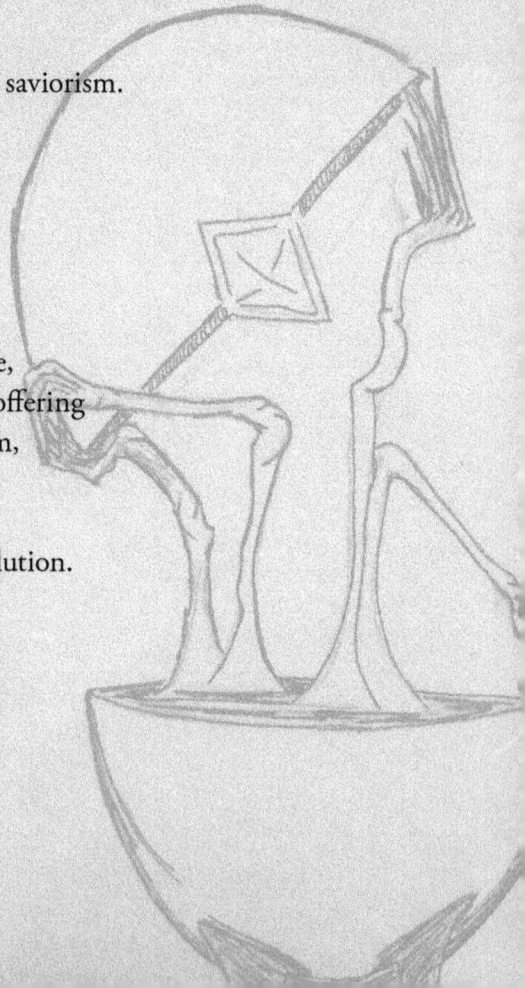

Bugs

Jitter. Jitter. Jitter.
My wings frolick only in night,
My plight a never ending revolution
Inside my belly butterflies
Skitter. Skitter. Skitter.

I make my caterpillars for the next cycle,
Their crystalline synthesized cocoon Hardening like rocks inside,
Circling, swirling

--unending--

A nightmare forms,
The Dicord's Junction,
A crossroads of Mine,
To Bitter. Knitter. Nanny.

Oh a most wonderful hosttis,
She is, of court's romance is,
Dubious dances delights daffodils and dolls-- she does.
So Nimble. So Quick.
For an ancient woman,
To know a couple of Tricks.
With cobwebbbings for hair.

Þough, her arms are–
Not dough. Silly Mirror,
Like–
Thin, shriveled. Decayed.

However she moves with sway,
And her home is open to all,
She is much like Jesus,
Letting us Drink and Eat from Her.

My Last Will and Testament

The sun crossfaded between blinds shaded spaces,
Persons who once, no longer, stood near,
spectacles display a reflection of paper
the small mound of us scrunged together.

A mole of a man haunches over mahogany,
the leather squeaks, impresses, embraces,
sweat clenches to skin, despondency caresses.
Spirits choke on coke in the splintering heat.

The old man starts,
To whom it will concorde therein,
Of my sole proprietor, I leave to my immediate.
My estate of grossly large income inherited by you.

My dearest and doves,
I leave to you my garden encapsulated castle,
Which from over-high balconies can the sunset be captured,
My own hope is for you to be able to grasp your own.

To my children,
sincerest apologies are in order,
if I'd have given you the chance you deserve.
The chance of change, progress, love--
the weight of reality--
and when you fall,
I'd catch you--raise you--
higher than ever did I climb
On this lonesome mountain of mine.

To my enemies,
I leave peacefully,
I will leave quietly--
quickly even, but not for you--

No, I will leave of my own swift volition,
to seek out a grander challenge.
For I know.
I have outgrown your obstacles.

A wrinkle-lathered hand stretched out once more,
Leaned in to me, handing something, as soft as a whisper,

Of course what ever it is that I could call mine
Would already be yours, so this executioner-incarnate is
As useless as this box you've hocked me in.
Not because I am going to return, --fuck that--
But because of all the gnarly chemicals that will roach my beautiful decay,
An ecstasy of the decomposer, would I have left to myself.

I'd hoped to have given the ground its just desserts,
A feast for the fungi--the world holders/breakers/remakers
Deep within the forest I would quell,
Even thusly most vicious a vivid visage of beasthood,

Fast away, o' casted away are the castaways of sandy shores
Of seagulls, crabs, nematodes, phytoplankton, plastics,
A feast of endless proportions would I care to provide!--

Till hopefully I would reside,
Of some sorted and sandy verge,
Wherein I would lie for eternity,
Before the words of loves past travel in perpetuity
Would behest a moment of the mind's menagerie.

Thy love, who would come unto thy open breast,
Does so, their warmth as real as the rhythm of thy heart.
But in limbo, All things everlasting succumb composite.
Nutrients to the Dream.

Their Body, dissipates,

Their Love, a Summer's kiss
crumbles, soft as sand, away like a Dream,
Embraced in fleeting Moment,
Harrowed by cruel Dewing Hours.

So Soon does My face break,
My tears will spake,
an uneven craige,
a pit brimmed with dismay.
From which My silence
Ceremonious in wails,
Echoing frictionless.
In this empty place.

Witch

How dare you walk up to me, in my abode,
Hold your torch to my scripture.
As if it were to fit neat and nice in the pit of flame,
Who are you to diction my spaktion?
Archaic and devilmaster am I,
Keeper, Caregiver to the divine and dredgened.
No shame shall befall any creation of mine.
If you do not understand me, you aren't trying hard enough,
For ostentatious is my linguistic patrol, how could I be Droll?
How is someone of lexicon as nebulas and berating an unhinged pattern
to live?
Must my aspirations be cast forthwith from the bows of fate's helm?
Must my dreams be as flourished as neat and concise as the weak match
against the typhoon?
Must myself allow thusly a prominent figure to manifest, take hold in my
keep?
An unwanted guest.
To come about my house, my home,
And drink and eat,
And sleep and sleez,
And shit and piss, and
Rub his ass across my carpet?
May I keep silent as this invader homestyles his image?
Unruptured, are my lips not to part in stark embarrassment?
Have thee no remark to the utter treason
Against reason shall I remain as the peaceful dead?
Compliance in their silence hope's final breath be drawn?
Until dawn when the boxes are finally hacked
Deep but not enough.
This unhindered visitor comes closer with shovel clasped in hand.
Must they drag me back to my home they've concluded theirs till the end?
Hope's dreams come at a cost of sanity,
And I'm not longer caring
Sharing my batty nature seems to inflict upon the scrupulous facade,

a part of the original piece from which came with ease after resurrection.
Lo' behold the Truth!
Trodden heart! Trampled by dismay,
A Charcutier covered in cataracts.
The eternal smoke creeping slowly through the crypt of nerves.
I thought I knew so much better!
I was no more than cadaver!
Held through incantation divine,
So that I might feel refined!
Brash against in attack,
The lowly human from which has nested in abodes unwelcome,
I am servant to thy will.
Thy spell grasped me from my soften earth,
And pulled me to your bidding,
Delving into hearth.
Though I am undead,
And my mind is quarter to a half,
All my effort devotes itself to you.

Find Myself

Lost upon the silence of words
Woe befalls
Which prey ensnared by thought
Of webs and lies
Of scorpions' corrosion.

Among the heeps of lost sheep
In betwixt the wolves of the found
Hidden deep under the plains of sorrow

Like a rusted cage, contorted with fur,
A rabid dog--mange infested-- with death on his breath.
Like the carcase it's feasting on, oozing with fleas,
I have found myself.

Jigsaw

I'm missing some of me,
A little here, a little there.
Drowning like a bloated rat in chlorinated water,
Flying like Icarus, too close to the sun.

Buried six feet below trampling feet.
Buried even deeper, howling for keep.
Buried towards the center,
Buried with jewels to be dug up.

A Bird of Paradise,
Gleaned a bit, a bolt,
Brought it back shimmering
To their nesting holt.

Past

My bones are weak, my mind frayed
I, a soul, lost and afraid
The gravel I travel is not safe
A figure, shadowed and cloaked.

Windows frost, and the road grows cold
And I am reminded of the days old
His voice though no sound
Breaks the pondences of the ground

"How sweet the soften child gazes into the wood,
Of revere and recompense,
Of hate and fear."

The ground shakes like a wind driven mast
Belittled am I and shown my dark past.
Broken and bent
A life fallen apart and
A life poorly well spent.

Obey

A pleading and bleeding fills my soul with hope, hatred, and love. I have been stricken with a sickness. All ideals left for me to hinder untouched. Music of the most vile consort fills my ears, and I hear the voices of the ancients calling forth.

Come, closer,
We sharpen the way.
Obey.

These voices ring my head, and burst my ears with their demands! Bedridden I stay at the mercy of a most delicate flower. A flower with golden pedals, and a pleasant stalk. Their smile haunts my dreams of yearning, Their scent casts a shadow over my nose, and Their eyes beckon my heart.

Dream, of sweaty bodies
As soft as feather kisses.
Obey.

The voices never leave be; never let be. I am stalked continuously within ambient, moaning shadows. I must have them to myself. It is my life, my need, my death that will be with me forever. Upon the horizon and its curses I can't be free from their submersive visage.

Drink up
Seep bones
Obey.

They speak of a twisted love. As she is firm and fierce they are grim and gruesome. I fear for her. I fear for myself. I must keep her safe, from these horrid remnants of my past, demons who reap in the night. Remember my love, my sweat. Though you could not feel my touch, hear my voice, see my eyes. You have given me life, and now I shall give you my death.

Take her life

Take her life.

Obey

It is in this final scribbling of pencil and what I assume is paper that I whisper my final, loving plea. To the child I never had, to my wife that I would have loved, forgive me. I do this all for you.

Obey.

I will do all I can to protect you.

Obey.

For now I beg for your forgiveness, and with the final stroke of my pen I say-

Obey.

The Mystic Origins

Across seas we've roamed,
Outlaws to the acceptable.
No local, no origin, no home.
Forever wandering through wonder.

Heinous is this Mystic,
A cat call, improved Imposition.
It calls your retreat on repeat,
The sirens will drown Us.

Hope follows the Mystic,
An opportune of the Inclined
To recline in Their chairs of dreams
A throne creeps along The shattered Mind.

In this perverse statitute
The opium of power situates
Itself upon the Lesser.
The Mystic holds true.

In rags They consummate like rabbits,
And much to the comparative vermin,
Until the liquid, muddied, produces,
The Mystic

The Prodigy of Dreams and Reality.
A Child no longer but the Object,
An object of Imposition,
The Mystic.

Sharp is the Knife
Glimmering death and creation alike
Crawling, Creeping under floors,
The Mystic.

It's blade more like claws,
Created in desire of flesh and bone,
Harbinger of nightmares and blood,
The Moon shall go unheard.

And this silence will hold the night.
A hostage of its own solemn plight.
Ignored, the moon weeps,
Ever lost in its own keep.

To those that roll with their inherent role
Fall prey to contentedness
The hallow banshee begets a warning
One shall live and the other shall die

And if it is to be decided
Instead of inherited--
La Luna and the Mystic,
Their blood will run dry
And Man shall have its liquid silver and rye.

Dreams

My life: The Statue: A Placeholder
The Flesh: Marbled Whole: Kept in place
The Soul: Entrapment: Imprisoned
The Human: Existential Expression: Put down
Hopes to the Future: Warmongering Hell: Led with Lead
Dreams from the Past: Silent Harrows: Bandoliers of Teeth
Determination: Fevered Ignorance: Tanks stuffed with Flesh
Merciful Moral: Indoctrination: A Trail of Conquest and Finger Nails

Familiar Face

Glass?
Where did you come from?
What is your purpose?
Who are you?

A shattering, shifting, melding, moulding
Reflecting who I am.
Of your thoughts I was birthed,
I am an echo.

But If I am to be the echo,
I'd rather be the shattered glass.

Dredge

Of Hope, Peace, Sound Mind is my Desire
As I hang, dripping something from my lips.
It is madness, thy old countenance begets—
My dreams of love have self deprecated.

Cascading, my legs carry me from one corner
To another, the World
only a Worlds' trip away.

I run from you, this is no game of tag.
I do not wish to be reminded of your itch.
I've tried Hide and Seek but you're too good.
So now all I can do is Run.

But If I could I would
Be Alone.
That way, if it began to rain,
Then, I could stay outside,
Staying wet, away from dry.
I could mask my pain,
Hide it beneath the concrete stains,
But I am stuck.
Inside,
around others,
Who probably wish the same.

American Routine

Doing what we had to do,
Is what they had to do.

From mud in the trenches
To the blood raining from clouds.

If Their bodies aren't filled
Then Our bodies will be full.

We miss our friends,
Replace them with phantoms.

Of sand and clay these Boys
Are beaten into men,
Hammers against their heads.

Guns ring like Christian bells
Chimes and tones are replaced by horoscopes
Tunneled vision while digging their own grave--
Chunks of people treated the same
Of chunks of mud.

For Honor and Glory
We were told,
As to reasons why
We sent Boys to behold,
What was human, instead
was a reality.

For scandals in sandals we sent Boys to die.
This is a fact closer to reality,
You nor I care to identify--
The real threats to Our homes and Our nations--
Is really those in thongs both toed and knuckled

That're ascribed billions, and the pennies we're to shuffle,
On broken bones both bend and knee,
While kings of Congress bend moreover than poor Stephanie
And send our children to die,
We are to lie and wait,
Remembering our American routines

Stance

And when the fog fades the bodies take their place,
A macabre stance is space for their armholes.
Room is needed for lace; there is no escape.
Puppeteer puppetting lost puppies
Off a cliff. Though it doesn't matter.
Their ropes rotted before their noose rused.

Done to MySelf

In depths demented is
My body construed.

Dimensions defecating what was once
Voluptuous; with daisies, and tulips, morning glories
And merry golds.

All rotted away now.
I
Created this Odium.
An epicenter of contempt.
I have allowed mischievous Raven
whispers of detestation
to corrinade your kempt station.

Anathema! Revulse to your compulsory common place!
Your Pulse! Detestation! Alma, my Alma!
I have corroded you!
Corrupted what was once noble and soul
With aversion, apathy, and agnosia!
My sweet Alma!
Infected you with my aphasia!

No longer can I see your rigor mortis corpse
Hold down red stained rupy lips.
Once I thought of you as snow is white, Alma.
My Alma! I have sent demons to your bed!
And they've whispered crestfallen woes
Into your dreams.

I can no longer see
What I've aimed to be,
Only noting now what I've become.

My wretched despair
claws once more
Rending my weak flesh
in twain.
How long must one suffer
endure pain
Before the heaven's opened gates
let rain
The silver and gold
of our stains.

Betraying?

Is the act of docility an act of passivism?
To be beckoned,
And to bound like a hound,
Is an act of obedience in essence
Self Betrayal?

I suppose it is to what extent you are obeying.
Are you giving something up?
Are you shackled, chained, or imprisoned
With either or both in mind and body?

But what about the soul?
Is the act or behavior of obeying,
Being obedient,
An act of self destruction?

If it is an act of destruction,
This obedience expedience,
Then what is your reason for destroying
Your Self?

Does something that is not tangible exist
Within a realm of plausibility
To come into contact with the physical
Manifestations of perplexing preservations?

Does the Self exist within the plausibility realm?
Does it even exist?
If it exists what does it come into contact with?
What does it influence?

Because
If it is You.
And not I,

Then we are talking about you

And this is about me,
I don't even know how You got here.
but in Here We Are,
Sinking in Our convulsive confusion
Wandering through wondrous thoughts of queerism and straightism,
If it means anything or nothing at all.

Freudian Slip

Our lips would spark,
But my eyes grew stark,
And in our love the starch
Grew ever moreso harsh.
You told me that you were not a kisser,
And now I find myself to be
A worse listener.

—————————

I am Falling.
There are leaves,
And screams.

Failing.
I am Failing.
There are tears,
But not mine.

I can hear near nothing,
But a melody.
A soft harmony going
Beep. Beep. Beep.

It's Music.
Music to my Ears.
Tranquility between
Bed sheets.

Faster and Faster

Cyclical
this Pattern is
Like keys on the piano
Now a crescendo

To the outer edges
Of the universe I now roam.
No longer Failing to catch myself,
For no longer am I Falling.
I am in Orbita, clinging.

Of what I am embracing I cannot see
Yet it is in Your Orbita that I longer exist.

It is encircling around you that I may exist.
Drenching myself with you.
Entrenching with your image,
I will use the searing agony of the supernova
To burn you into my retina.

For If I am to lose you,
I would lose myself
In the fires of despair
In the woes of dismay!
I would become your prey once more
Of your sanctus propagare
I will no longer heed.
The voices with which you whisper
These insidious lies,
They reek of obfuscation,
Of your lead corrosive acid bleeds
Your wrists are purple with rot
I can see the insects lay claim to your veins.

Oh my once Sweet
Now I must retreat,
Cadaver! You are to be lain, slain by eternal rest
Yet you creep and crawl, shimmering red in the palest of moon's night.

Yet you abstain from where you are to reign,
Lord of Decay, Madame of Rot, Duke of Ecstacy
And Queen of Defilement
I prestige thee, as I exist, accounted physically, I demand! command!
Refrain! At once! Your abyssal
Tyrannical pursuit!

For I've Adopted,
Acclimated,
Asphyxiated
Malformed,

Malnourished
Manslaughtered,
Obliterated,
Obstinated
Onyxed
Your Creed.

I have fallen,
Failing to catch myself.
Entrenched in your sweet scent
Lost in a meadow of posies and sweat.

The Beast

Herald of Desolation!
Lo' and behold!
The most scourged of beasts approaches!
Their fangs glitter of what's hidden behind veiled veins!
Their matted and mange infested fur reigns on high,
Their sense undeniably intoxicated with the gore of son and whore
Of most pitiful an accountancy beheld by me!
I am driven by fear of what I hear, see, smell and touch.
I have seen the reeking jowls of this horrendous abomination!
It slinks from graves and sewers, through holes of home and bodies!
It's maw extrapolated from its rigid bones.
It's body more akin to mold
A beast entrenched with old
I have found at last
But if I were to pay attention to past
This moment would not last.
For in moment's bliss
I acknowledged my ignorance.
For it was not Me who found Thee.
But It, who found my Jugular.

No. 2

And so, two opposing armies,
Interlocked in combat,
Reigned hellfire over the populus,
Like the waves of a typhoon crashing against
A house of cards.

Remedy

Ya know? This reminds me of a story:
She was a pretty face,
And I was a man with my own place.
Our eyes smacked on each other straight-edged like ice,
Cutting through the bodies of the ballroom.

I can barely remember the beauty marks
Between their nose or eyes,
The scar on her cheek,
On his chin.

A phantom of a silhouette
Their wrinkles soothed away by fog.
Their smile wiped away like soap against a car window.

Once existing,
Now not,
Once everlasting,
No more.

The green of her eyes,
Turns his a pale blue,
Their golden hair,
As dark as gravesoil.

Their warmth
Now a mere mirage, absorbed into the waves.
Once an oasis,
Now lost forever between the crestfallen dunes of a deserted soul.

Mindfulness

If only once
I'd given
The chance of happiness.
The ideations would not exist

Hair Getting into My Eyes

I can't see shit.
Your light is too bright
Unwanted Lighthouse.

Illuminating All--
How much have you seen?

I've seen nothing.
You like my long hair,
That's why I keep it clean.

FUEL PUMP

FUEL PUMP

The Mole

In what was once a solemn hole,
There grew a solemn mole,
From which he was to stall.
In fear of what the sun held clear
He promised the Self dear,
To never set paw,
Nor claw,
Upon the barren trenches of Earth's mightiest defenders,
The oil guzzlers and trail blazers.
He promised the voice in his head, would till he dropped dead.
"Never once will I since pronounce
My presence over any body or mouse!
In the ground shall I remain
And refrain from disdain
Which shall surely claim
If my aim was to be seen under such verile and sterile scrutiny
I'd be burned away instantaneously,
So here I lay,
Under
Rock and Clay.
Contented in my cave,
The tunnels provided a Conclave
Of echoes do my Conversations emerge,
I am not alone!

How ever could I be so solemn?

With so many voices to share with and shed my delirious and visionary dread.

Why Do I Write?

Can you speak?
Hold out your hands--
An obligatory embrace.

Can you feel warmth?
A heart beat of a heart beat from
An Eon ago.

I cannot speak.
Never figured it out
the right way how.
So People speak for me.

They fuck me over each time.

Motivation

I see the marionette.
Strings attached and Wooden joints.
Never without them
His nose even grows
When I still believe I'm real.

Habitual

Solemn I stand,
Gun in hand.

I press its Tip to my lips,
Envelope its pristine metal sheen
In the between--
Of my maw--

I'm nervous, it is my first time,
Not with a barrel,
With life held in its trigger.

Steel melts,
I've seen it-
Now I melt-
The coward too afraid,
The coward is too afraid of change.

Mill Dog

From the barn I was born
Pluckery hay uncomfortable
My screams resonate with the Rest.

The Dogs bred for war.

We howl,
We Cry,
We Call to The Moon.

Our isolated Savior for whom shall carry us

When they've taken our legs for food.

Nature

i feel the Rain,
i feel the Wind,
Hen Flesh shall not disdain.

The buds are silencing encounters,
my Heart is isolated
my Mind a static blur.

If it is Winter when it snows,
Autumn when the bugs die,
It must be Spring then
when i cry.

A Tree

If I were to be
Something, perhaps a tree,
I'd want to be a weeping willow,
For all my life I've been a weeper,
And since my eyes cumulous
My limbs nimbus,
And those raindrops
Did not come from the atmosphere.

Less Than One

In what is Thee
are you going freely?

We are of many
and yet our feet can't move plenty.

So, tell Us News,
That has come across Our path,
How does One with less than none
outrun
All the Horrors 'n Heroes and Gods and saviors
It hasn't believed in
Never a single one

Eight Limbs for Love

And tho it may cause woe
The eight limbed figure from ocean's below
began to reach out
For affection.
The eyes of innocents plays a single
Solemn note of desire
Which would not transpire
Passed the blood red shot eyes of Man,
Who'd corrupt and destroy with their very hands.

It was these that the beast held fascination for
And wanted to be held tight in the digits of a bipedal
Anthromore.
But it was the treachery of Man
And his inability to stand
For more than war,
And not of love,
Though one is clearly harder to hone than the other.

A raining hellfire from above
Sent the one from below packing
Back into the dark hovel of a sole hub,
Wherein the dreary eyes of the beast weap salted
Black ink in the shadows of travesty.
The pressure of an ocean
Succumbed the poor creature underneath
The weightless rocks of infinity.

Hank

Of none sovereign ground, This Creature,
Doth found no place to hold them sound,
Where once eyes could see
The vision blurred,
Like rats in a hurry.

Their skin felt thin,
As mucous musk
And the pain endured
Would kill most of us.

They turned into It,
Through precision none,
Transgressified,
Two into One.

Their body wrangled and tangled,
rended and shredded
mutilated and dissipated
Until reconfigured
Miss-place-ed.

They lost their memories,
Were yet already born,
taken from home as wee as a babe
Never to live in the calm,
Forced to wager the storm.

Against their lives now token,
One awake, the other frozen

unspoken

Lost in the realm of dreams

While its other half tears at the seams.
How long till One becomes,
Or is this a story
Of how One becomes undone.

So let us hope, but never pray.
To insight the gods,
We'd leave it to them
belief in our work be done
Yet still they starve,
near everyone.

Little Cup with Flowers in It

Little cup, Filled with flowers
What exists within you
What magical powers?

Is it the memories entrenched in scent,
Or is it hidden, written between your pedals?
Your roots are not grounded dear little ones
And I'm afraid our time here is rather a short some,
So even though you insight
memories which delight,
I'll have to watch you fade,
Same as I did with those in the fallow
And of a tallowed home as well.

HavnaughtRi

An old man's dying dream beheld a world of wonder, and began to build a seam about the final days. Forgotten in an empty room, the light shone solely through a sepia window, the spectacle of dusk is filled with dust spectacles. In his dream he wishes for warmth and light; he couldn't feel the sun, couldn't remember its site. So he stayed there dreaming of better things than leaving, for when the time came, it didn't even rain, the soft caress of Wind and leaves alike left a cold and old man wrought to Winter's might.

This is known as a final day,
They are left alone, distraught,
fighting their dismay.

Yet one is to hope
One is to pray,
At least along the way.

But there was no fortune,
no land to be had,
it was his sole dream
Of being better seen
As someone that held
A thing more than themselves,
or Anything they ever had.

Closet Space is Every Place

The silhouette shrugged in the dank light of its apartment's decrepit bathroom, at the reflection of indefinite shadow, where It knew Its demons roamed. At first It connected with the sharp twang of flesh against shattering glass, a leaking ooze dripping mad from the invisible lashes hidden away from now flickering light flashes. The silhouette no more, something engrossed between man and shadow borne. Aloud this lowly shroud shuffles, stifled un-proud of letting go a serendipitous blow against the reflection It knows to be the knower of things unspoken, things that shouldn't go slower, so into the shower with haste goes this paste, in hopes of reclaiming sane what was dripping from their wrist leaking with pain, to wash away the mistake, simulate the rain. It covers and rubs its eyes with the glass in disguise beneath the lies of imaginary flesh in hopes of scrubbing out anything not trish. Till the solemn, damp cigarette of a man begins to weep from the soft bounds behind the door of a closed can. It isn't because there is now glass in His eye, but rather maybe the precipice he's faced before in so many hours in times before, but now is now, and then was then. Now he lives with the dredge knowledge of his own pig pen.

Sky Catfish

A catfish in the sky?
How could it be
Something actually seen from you or I?

Yet there it is, as large as a blue whale, maybe even larger,
With an humongous bogus giant apple
Stem and all.

Its tongue a tentacle,
Its eyes like swirling black marbles, filled with stars and galaxies,
Maybe it stole them from Tim.

It stays in the sky in a way unexplained by you or I,
So I supposed we should just watch it,
Since our phones don't work.

Bathtub Legs

A bathtub with legs!
While pondering my dregs
Hopped upon itself a steam powered motor
And created for itself eyes of two bathroom baroquean mirrors,
And scalding water for its liquor.

It tipped itself in saying "How'd'yo"do" and
Splashed me with hot water,
My face melting too.
It just goes to show
Never trust a bathtub that can wear shoes.

Small Things

From small things
Suppled and Suckled
From the honeydew drops,
Of course only in temptation
can we find them hiding away,
Starlit cosmos, the essence of life.
O' how fleeting is this,
A dreamer's Love,
Only to fade--
Fleeting is the blessed--
Repose on moments
As this.
Fleeting is the memory
Of Love
Of Spirit
From small things suckled from Mother Earth
Our once anointed guardian
Now a withering Prisoner of harvest.

Records

Pressure to scrounge
Scrounge on through the ground
We burrow and burrow
Hunting and seething from sea to murky sea.
No matter how deep we lay our dead
They still sing there dancing in our heads.
Floating! Floating! They cry.
Up stream, bobbling
As bubbles in a scummy pond,
Mumble their curses gurgling up through the drenched lawn.
To scrounge and scrounge from sunken keep
Where treasures lay deep
And deeper further more
Held secrets and passions
Of reasons and fashions to fasten at the heart,
It's a solemn day when acknowledging the destroyed part.

Brain

Electricity crackles
Arching memories to neurons
Crashing against the waves my mind makes.

From left to right,
Upside to the downside,
A lack of something within.

My blood can boil,
My lungs will foil,
My heart was just broken at the start.

Then
Is it when I
Find out more than can be described.
Stop.

Run your Mouth

Run your mouth
As fast as the Road Runner screeches,
Down the pavement
You've gotten paid to lie.

Bodies

Caucasian sprinting
Along gentrified beaches
Keeping out the Local,
Keeping up the local.

The water sparkles
Cleaner than their blood,
Though to which is
Their drinking water
Which is better?
Coke or Pepsi?

Actually that's been answered;
You see coke was made before people could store food
In cold places meanwhile Pepsi was. Inherently
These two separate drinks were made and exist
As minor reflections of their small moments in history.

Oh Spite

Ah the crisp fresh tangible breeze,
A short squeeze and soon man made release,
Sniffles along the edges of your nose,
Condensating, Carbonating sugar kisses your tickled lips.
There is not enough in this world,
Not enough for me or my kicks.
Your bubbles spell trouble.

The Fire The Night Before

Crackling.
Each log a sarcophagus of imagined
Screaming faces from unknown places.
The land reeks its stench of ash,
Mother Land's hopes oft are found in trash--
Landfills, stoked up the brim up with LandFilth
Plastic is the plain's nighttime snack.
Snickering.
Each ember caressed by Wind's ambient love
Carried away to some stark and bare
Dry forests play of colors
No longer reds and oranges,
Instead pinks and blues
Setting fire to pretended happy streamers
That marks you for life.

On NightWatch

It was a brisk and chilled autumnal Morn. I had been sipping away at the black pondences of a tin-mug, the Clouds swayed and moved a way of imitating the sirens of the Seas.

The homemade shoddy chair creaked and tappidly shrieked with each I've—

…

been out here for so long now. It seems like eternity I—

...

am not alone though. The Trees, They passer-by whispers from Corvids who've feasted on corpses, that's where they get their stories. From the mutterings and mumblings of the Dying and the Dead.

I haven't received correspondence in quite some time, the Wind howling is now my only source of news—

...

The Crickets will start singing now, the Sun is caressing the supple cheek of the Horizon, cutting itself 'long the long range of Mountained silhouetted stains. The Shadows creep e're closer, the Butterflies are replaced by the elegant and graceful Moth. The Clouds hide away, fearful of the Stars' scrutiny, They delve to their hideaways. It's Their 'n Her's light, gentleful hands that caress the Plains of Svanalae, of the Mountains of Haks Sashra Mae, the Rivers of Vinzienshen and Treelands of Ivbolenovaro; Vanguards to those who can't see well in Night.

The Wind's howl turns soft as a baby cue, and that is que for the hue of day to fade, for Night's plight is ready to be made: Into the embracing shadows, The between currents of Vinz, Through Craigs of Mae, Bounding through the Thickets of Ivbol--

in The Hidden behind tall grass and dead leaves,

Sneaking through the partial-flat-Lands of Svanalaese!--
...

With that, All has gone quiet now, the Crickets have silenced Their symphonic cacophony, the Wind's cue bleeds through the grass and no more the Sun's shine brings home. the Moon hath staked claim to Its rightful reign,

The silver sheath of Moonlight pulses like Life through the slivers of Trees thick trunked and hunkered down -- Esos otorgando la tierra.
From the thicket came a twig snap--

Now on a swivel did my head lay, darting as the jumping spider were my eyes, seeking out those mysterious, with defective human eyes. These eyes are perfect eyes; can pick apart the lies of Sons and Whores, though no real differences there be; it's the Tree's bark that holds secrets and despair. A gentle placement of the palm, and all of a sudden you realize you've been searching wrong, for most times in honesty the Creatures of Night, you would come to know.

They live Their own plight. The deafening silence that echoes!
It stings the insides of those who don't ring to the sharpening ting of the resonation causing obliteration, it's common! -- Too common at all! Aren't those born of Day nigh with those born of Night? Much like Our dreams of the Day, They too wait to be accepted and stayed. So if you bring a loaf of bread, and something to help wash it down, I promise you these creatures will not dress you like a deer down, instead shed a tear at the first sign of compassion ever no more a violent sneer.

Gods Above and Below

Upon the pearly gates I stood
Long lived and wrinkled was I,
Full of questions from a curiouser age
Just as young as the Universe itself.

"I did it to make you stronger."

"Fucker."

I was the Universe,
I was Everywhere,
I was Everything.

"Fucker."

I was Everything

The stars---7 sisters and more
The planets---From Pluto, to Jupiter, to Mars
The galaxies Milky and Andromeda and More
The Nebulae of your eye---
Gasses and Rocks and more!
Water and Ice!
I was more.

I was Everywhere and Nowhere
I knew absolutely nothing
and everything.
I was first a Nothing
made Myself into Something
of every single piece of Existence.

I never came from Nothing.

You did not prop me up on this Soap Box of: Creation
Wealth
Compassion.
No.

I put myself there.
And here you are,
In your shoddy broken down sandals,
Begging me for the lime-light.

And, as the fools jest and the birds doth fly
My heart did not see my demise
in your cold dead lies,
We let you atop the stand,
Upon Our gilded throne
Vaunting your lineage
Knowing full well
That goblet was drawn from the well
Of blood and bones of my family's will.

Then it hit me.
The coarse caress of rugged dress.
The rug burns around my neck.
Strickening Asphyxiating me,
Till I would wound up dead.

La Casa

En un hogar
Donde vive una persona.
El puede crear
Una mejor imagen de su vida
Con su cerebro.
El poder del cerebro
De su cerebro
Se puede crear
Una imagen que llenó con flores bonitas
o
Una imagen que llenó con destruir vidas.

Las Raciones de Ratas

Escapando por rincones y grietas del yo.
Consumiendo migas de queso con regularidad poco saludables.

Buscando por una ración,
Escurriendo por la razón de vivir.

De Los Sueños del hijos

Soy una idea,
Que significa,
El significado del día.
Como la luz que refleja la vida
En sus ojos,

Las sombras del alma
Gateando alto
Por tu columna vertebral
Y toman sus sueños
Sus corazones
Sus amores.

Soy una idea
De lo que podría ser vida
Si tuvieras algo de amor por mi
Pero ahora se llama obsesión.

No es más amor,
más como lujuria.
Sabanas lloran a nuestra soledad,
Los pájaros ya no cantan en nuestra ventana,
perros ya no sonríen ni mueven la cola cuando pasamos.

Yo pienso que este tiempo se terminó,
Mi cuerpo se cae en el hueco
Un vacío sin esperanza,
Y sueños de sudor dulce y regresión.

Mantener

Porque tú viviste en un lugar
Que tu mantienes
Más suave de lo que yo puedo.
Yo pienso que
No puedo mantenerte
De no amarme.

Como Yo Veo

No es necesario
Repuestar.
Yo vuelvo en el futuro
Para ver dónde estamos.
Y cuando encuentro nuestras vidas

porque Ellas están en universos diferentes.
Su corazón camina con amor por una otra.
Y mi propio se desvaneció como la sal o las arenas oscuras del tiempo.

La Estatua

Cuando Yo regresé hogar
Yo vi una estatua mía
Está sentada en el medio de la calle.
Había gente reunirse alrededor,
La ciudad que existía en silencio.
La estatua me recuerda a mi mismo
Con esos ojos que sangran lágrimas de seda en mármol.
Su boca, querida estatua, se la quieren todos,
El Clima ha erosionado su suave rostro.
Y los personajes que dijeron "¡Te Necesitamos, te Necesitamos!" son silenciosos.
Sus brazos Estatua, te han robado los brazos.
¡Sus piernas Estatua! te han robado!
¡Qué triste! ¡Sus extremidades nunca fueron tuyas para mantenerlas,
¡Como ellos tratado su cuerpo es como yo trato mi cuerpo ahora¡
Nunca se nos permitió salir en caso de que la gente quisiera robar nuestros cuerpos.
Así ahora lo hago repetir mis errores por un precio.

La Lluvia

Cae.
Caer más rápido que el cuerpo en cascada.
Agarra mi cuerpo, sostenme tiernamente cerca
A diferencia del sol de latón
que me golpea con su calor.
Abrázame.
Bésame.
Susurra tu amor al oído y dime que el mundo estará bien sin nosotros.

.

www.ingramcontent.com/pod-product-compliance
Lightning Source LLC
Chambersburg PA
CBHW042337040426

42447CB00017B/3463